The Rotary Club of Urbana is pleased
to donate this book to the
Urbana Free Library in honor of:

# CHILDREN
## AROUND THE WRLD

by
## Joanna Brundle

Look out for blue words in this book. You can find out what they mean in the Glossary on Page 24.

# CONTENTS

We are going to visit lots of countries. Look at the map on Page 23 to find out where they are.

©2016
Book Life
King's Lynn
Norfolk PE30 4LS

ISBN: 978-1-78637-011-2

Written by:
Joanna Brundle

Designed by:
Ian McMullen

A catalogue record for this book is available from the British Library.

# FAMILY LIFE

THIS FAMILY IN ENGLAND ARE ENJOYING LUNCH TOGETHER.

Around the world, many children live with their parents and brothers and sisters. But there are lots of different kinds of families. Who do you live with?

In China, over half of all children live with their grandparents while their parents work.

UNTIL 2015, CHINESE PARENTS WERE ONLY ALLOWED ONE CHILD.

In some countries, like Cambodia, Costa Rica and Mexico, very large families with many children are common.

THESE CHILDREN IN INDIA HAVE TO LOOK AFTER THEMSELVES.

In some countries, it is usual for several generations to live together.

THIS FAMILY IN SUDAN ALL LIVE TOGETHER.

Families respect the older people, who help to bring up the children.

AN ASIAN GRANDMA HELPS HER GRANDSON TO MAKE CAKES.

7

# WHAT'S FOR BREAKFAST?

IN MANY COUNTRIES, CHILDREN ENJOY CEREAL AND MILK FOR BREAKFAST.

In Malawi, children eat cornmeal porridge with boiled potatoes for breakfast. In India, a cake called idli, made from lentils, is popular. Korean children eat kimchi, made of cabbage leaves.

# WHAT'S FOR LUNCH?

Do you have a lunchbox? Japanese children have special ones called bento boxes. Inside are animal faces, cartoon characters and patterns, all made from food like rice, seaweed and fruit.

SEAWEED

RICE

KIWI

# SCHOOL UNIFORM

School uniform looks very different around the world. How are these uniforms similar to and different from the one you wear?

TIBET

NEPAL

IRAN

CUBA

Masai people in Kenya and Tanzania wear cloaks called shukas.

MASAI CHILDREN

# TRADITIONAL CLOTHES

AN ALPACA

A CHULLO IS A TRADITIONAL HAT WITH EAR FLAPS.

A PONCHO IS A WARM CAPE.

In Peru, Quechua people dye wool from alpacas and use it to make clothes.

# TIME TO GO TO SCHOOL

How do you travel to school?

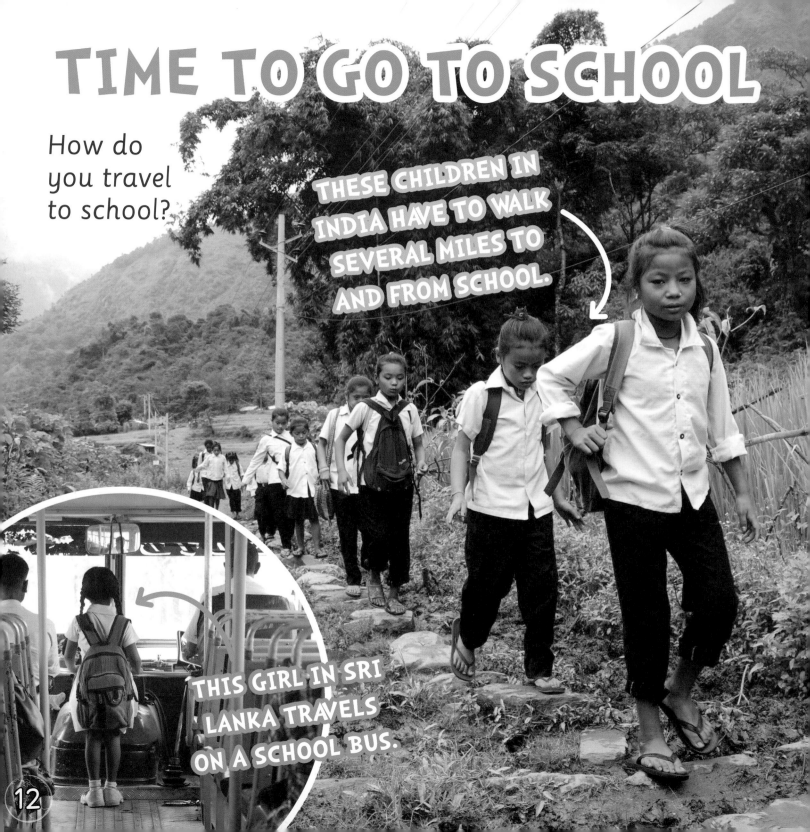

THESE CHILDREN IN INDIA HAVE TO WALK SEVERAL MILES TO AND FROM SCHOOL.

THIS GIRL IN SRI LANKA TRAVELS ON A SCHOOL BUS.

In Cambodia, the whole family rides on this motorbike. Only Dad gets a helmet.

A rickshaw takes these children to school in India.

13

# SCHOOL LIFE

There are many different kinds of school. This school in Uganda holds lessons outside.

IN NEPAL, THESE BOYS USE THE FLOOR AS A DESK.

In South Korea, children go back to school after supper and work through the evening.

A THAI BOY WORKING IN A RICE FIELD

But around the world, many children don't go to school at all. They have to earn money to help their families.

# PLAYTIME AND HOBBIES

Football is played all around the world. In poor countries, children play football. They make a ball by stuffing paper into plastic bags and wrapping rubber bands around it.

A BAREFOOT GAME IN KENYA

These children in Hungary are playing to win!

In the snowy mountains of France, Austria and Switzerland, children love to ski and snowboard.

In sunny Australia, surfing is a popular hobby.

# WELCOME TO MY HOME

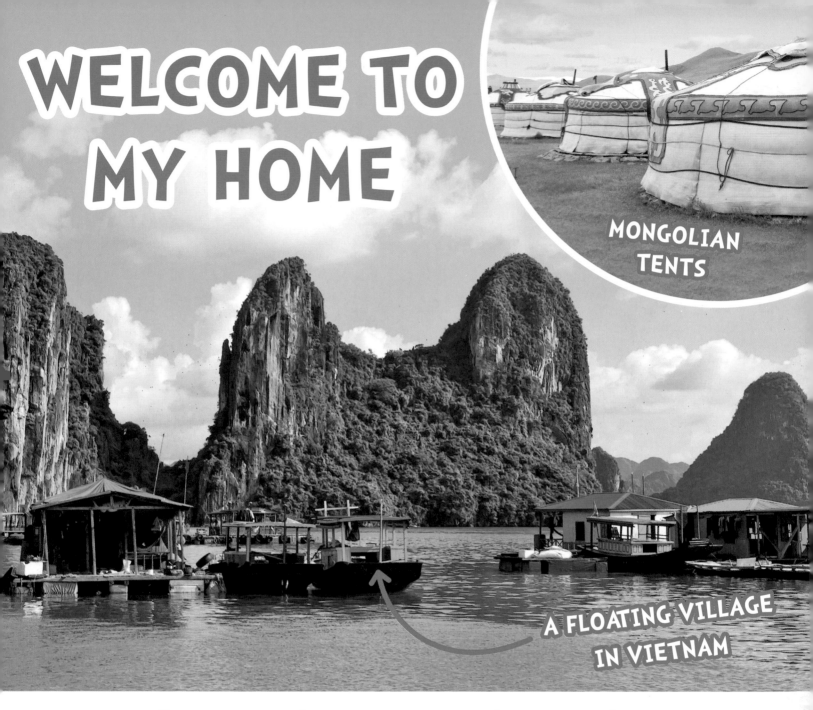

MONGOLIAN TENTS

A FLOATING VILLAGE IN VIETNAM

Houses, flats, tents, huts, caravans, boats and caves are all homes to children around the world.

Some children have been forced to leave their homes to escape danger. They are refugees and live in camps.

A REFUGEE CAMP IN TURKEY.

These children in Burkina Faso have no family to look after them. They live in an orphanage.

# ANIMALS AND PETS

Children love to keep animals as pets. In Japan, the golden hamster is the most popular. In Guatemala, children keep brightly coloured macaws.

RABBIT

GOLDEN HAMSTER

MACAW

CAN YOU GUESS WHICH PET IS MOST POPULAR IN THE UNITED KINGDOM?
(ANSWER ON PAGE 24)

Families also keep animals because they are useful. In Russia, this Nenet boy is dressed in reindeer skins to keep him warm.

In Vietnam, the water buffalo this boy is riding is used for ploughing. It is not a pet.

# TIME FOR BED

Not everyone has a comfortable bedroom like this to sleep in.

These boys in Nepal and Togo sleep on the ground.

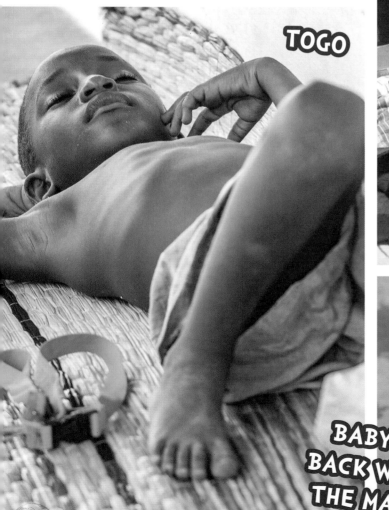

TOGO

NEPAL

BABY SLEEPS ON MUM'S BACK WHILE SHE WORKS AT THE MARKET IN VIETNAM.

22

# WHERE IN THE WORLD?

1. Europe
2. North America
3. South America
4. Africa
5. Australia
6. Asia

1. England
2. China
3. Cambodia
4. Costa Rica
5. Mexico
6. Sudan
7. India
8. Malawi

9. Korea
10. Japan
11. Iran
12. Tibet
13. Nepal
14. Togo
15. Cuba
16. Kenya

17. Tanzania
18. Peru
19. Sri Lanka
20. Uganda
21. Brazil
22. Thailand
23. Hungary
24. Australia

25. France
26. Austria
27. Switzerland
28. Mongolia
29. Vietnam
30. Burkina Faso
31. Turkey

# GLOSSARY

**GENERATIONS** Groups of people who are a similar age, for example grandparents, parents or children in one family

**MACAWS** Brightly coloured parrots with long tails

**ORPHANAGE** A place where children whose parents have died can live and be looked after

**PLOUGHING** Turning over soil with a machine called a plough, before sowing seeds

**RESPECT** To look up to someone and to care about their feelings and wishes

**ANSWER (PAGE 20) DOG**